Juni 1997

Für Fam. Ekholm,
in dieser wunderschönen Gegend der
Schweiz hält sich Debbie auf, umgeben von
schönen Bergen und Seen.
Hier bin ich auch aufgewachsen und
verwurzelt.
Zur Erinnerung an schöne Stunden
Margrit Egli

OSTSCHWEIZ

© 1996
Fotostudio und Alpsteinverlag
CH-9320 Arbon

Fotos und Text	Herbert Haltmeier
Titelbild	Bodensee mit Säntis bei Arbon/Steinach
Panoramakarte	Kettler, Meiringen
Gestaltung	Atelier Hofmann, Horgen
Fotolithos	Seelitho AG, Stachen/Arbon
Druck	AVD, Goldach
Einband	Burkhard AG, Mönchaltorf
Übersetzung	Intertext GmbH, Gais AR

Printed in Switzerland
ISBN 3-9521205-0-2

Herbert Haltmeier

The photographer, born in 1945, was just a ten-year-old schoolboy when he set up his first darkroom. Later, after training as a printer and working for various employers, he went into business on his own. Free-lance work for advertising and fashion photography followed, as well as studies of landscapes at home and abroad for the tourist trade during his travels. These pictures rapidly became very popular among publishing houses, photographic agencies and magazine editors. Further work included productions such as the "Ostschweiz" calendar (published annually since 1993), collaboration on the book "Switzerland", cover pages for magazines, books, postcards etc.

In addition to photography, Herbert Haltmeier employs his artistic talents in a number of traditional handicrafts involving various techniques. His pictures using handmade paper as a support are favourites at exhibitions. They include black and white photos, woodcuts, lithographs, water-colours and modern polaroid transfer photos. Here, once again, his motifs are people and places.

The photographs in this book were taken with several different cameras ranging from professional to miniature camera.

Landscapes are particularly demanding subjects, with the photographer having to carry up to 20 kg of equipment around with him. Weather and light conditions change rapidly; building sites, air pollution and other factors frequently spoil a good photo. Haltmeier spent 5 years accumulating pictures for this volume, taking some during hikes, some from the air and some even from a surf board.

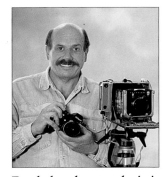

Herbert Haltmeier

Der Fotograf (Jahrgang 1945) richtete bereits im Alter von 10 Jahren als Schüler ein Fotolabor ein. Nach einer Lehre als Buchdrucker und einigen "Wanderjahren" folgte der Schritt zum eigenen Geschäft. Neben Werbe- und Modeaufnahmen entstanden durch die Reisetätigkeit für den Tourismus Landschaftsaufnahmen aus dem In- und Ausland. Diese Bilder waren bald begehrt von Verlagen, Bildagenturen und Redaktionen. Es entstanden Werke wie der Kalender "Ostschweiz" (erscheint seit 1993 jedes Jahr), Mitarbeit am Buch Switzerland, Titelseiten für Hefte, Bücher, Ansichtskarten usw.

Die künstlerische Tätigkeit umfasst neben dem Fotografieren weitere Techniken des traditionellen Handwerks. Auf handgeschöpften Papieren entstehen Schwarzweiss-Fotos, Holzschnitte, Lithografien, Aquarelle und moderne Polaroid-Transferbilder, die an Ausstellungen gezeigt werden. Auch hier sind die Sujets Mensch und Landschaft.

Die Bilder in diesem Buch entstanden mit professionellen Fach- als auch Kleinbildkameras. Landschaftsbilder sind sehr aufwendig, da bis 20 kg Ausrüstung mitgetragen wird. Wetter und Licht ändern sehr rasch, Baustellen, verschmutzte Luft usw. verunmöglichen vielfach ein gutes Bild. Auf Wanderungen, teilweise aus der Luft und sogar vom Surfbrett aus, wurde während 5 Jahren für diesen Bildband fotografiert.

Eastern Switzerland   Die Ostschweiz

The extremely beautiful region of Eastern Switzerland is framed to the north and east by the rich variety of scenery along the Rhine and Lake Constance. The canton of Schaffhausen with the famous Rhine waterfalls lies to the north-west.

Very early in history, the first settlers built their homes on the shores of these waters. Lake Constance supplies plenty of evidence from the era of the pile-dwellers. The Romans erected fortresses, the remains of which can be seen to this day, for instance in the castle of Arbon at the edge of the Lake. From here, you can see almost the whole of Lake Constance, the Alps extending from the Vorarlberg range all the way to the Grisons, and the striking view across the lake to the Säntis. The cover photo for this book was taken in the bay between Arbon and Steinach.

Because of its vast size, Lake Constance and its moods are forever changing. When the atmosphere is slightly hazy, the opposite shore cannot be seen and this is why the lake is also known as the "Swabian Sea".

The monastery and then the city of St Gall, later to become world famous for its embroidery, grew up around the hermitage of the Irish monk Gallus in the Steinach valley. Nowadays the area derives its prosperity from agriculture, modern industrial concerns, prestigious schools, hospitals and tourism. Right in the middle of Eastern Switzerland the remarkable range known as the Alpstein dominates the plateau. It is crowned by the Säntis. This mountain owes its significance as a meteorological observation station and radio transmitter to its unique situation. The tourist reaches the peak, 2503 m above sea level, either in comfort by taking the cable car or - for experienced mountain hikers only - on foot. The Alpstein and the Appenzeller Land are among the most popular areas for hiking in Switzerland. There is virtually no end to the number of trails and hikes, from easy strolls to strenuous climbs, or excursions by mountain railway, cable car and post bus. Again and again, you come quite unexpectedly upon breathtaking views, and there is always a good restaurant on the way or at your destination to make sure that you stay hale and hearty! The people of Appenzell are known for their hospitality, and their love of tradition lives on in their music and old customs. Here, folk culture is part of everyday life.

Following the Rhine Valley, the traveller reaches the Principality of Liechtenstein, which although politically independent, is touristically linked with Eastern Switzerland. The spa Bad Ragaz with the Tamina gorge lies in the upper Rhine Valley. Continuing on past Sargans, we come to the lake called the Walensee, reflecting the steep cliffs of the Churfirsten towering above. These distinctive peaks are also clearly visible from the Toggenburg.

From the village of Amden and the Kerenzerberg there is a lovely panorama extending right into the canton of Glarus, the most southerly canton of the tourist region defined as Eastern Switzerland. Our journey as recorded in this book ends in the long narrow valleys and high mountains that give this area its special charm.

Die wunderschöne Ostschweiz ist im Norden und Osten eingerahmt durch die abwechslungsreiche Landschaft von Rhein und Bodensee. Im Nordwesten liegt der Kanton Schaffhausen mit dem berühmten Rheinfall.

Schon früh wurde das Land an diesen Gewässern besiedelt. Am Bodensee findet man viele Zeugen aus der Zeit der Pfahlbauer. In der Römerzeit entstanden Festungen deren Zeugen heute noch stehen, wie z.B. das Schloss Arbon am See. Von hier erblickt man den grössten Teil des Bodensees, die Alpen vom Vorarlberg bis Graubünden und die wunderschöne Aussicht über den See auf den Säntis. In der Bucht Arbon/Steinach entstand auch das Titelbild zu diesem Buch.

Die Grösse des Bodensees lässt jeden Tag neue Stimmungen entstehen. Bei leichtem Dunst ist kein Ufer mehr zu sehen, so entstand auch der Name "Schwäbisches Meer".

Um die Einsiedelei des Mönches Gallus im Steinachtal entwickelte sich das Kloster und später die Stadt St.Gallen, die später durch die Stickereien weltbekannt wurde. Heute sind in der Ostschweiz Landwirtschaft, moderne Industriebetriebe, bedeutende Schulen, Spitäler und die Verwaltungen sowie der Tourismus die wichtigsten Einnahmequellen.

Mitten in der Ostschweiz ragt das einmalige Alpsteinmassiv mit dem Säntis aus dem Mittelland. Durch diese Lage ist dieser Berg von europäischer Bedeutung für Wetterbeobachtungen und Funkübertragungen. Der Tourist erreicht den 2503 m hohen Berggipfel bequem mit der Gondelbahn oder zu Fuss (nur für gute Berggänger). Der Alpstein mit dem Appenzellerland gehören zum beliebtesten Wandergebiet der Schweiz. Fast endlos könnte man hier wandern auf einfachen und schwierigen Touren, Ausflüge mit Bergbahnen und Postautos machen, alles ist möglich. Immer wieder wird man überrascht durch einmalige Aussichten, und gute Restaurants unterwegs und am Ziel sorgen für das leibliche Wohl. Die Appenzeller sind gastfreundlich und pflegen Tradition, Musik und Brauchtum. Hier wird Kultur auch im Alltag gelebt.

Durch das Rheintal gelangt der Reisende ins Fürstentum Liechtenstein, das touristisch mit der Ostschweiz zusammenarbeitet. Im oberen Rheintal liegt der Kurort Bad Ragaz mit der Taminaschlucht. An Sargans vorbei kommt man zum Walensee, der von den steilabfallenden Churfirsten geprägt ist. Diese Berge sind auch aus dem Toggenburg markant zu sehen.

Von Amden und auch vom Kerenzerberg aus fasziniert die schöne Panoramasicht ins Glarnerland immer wieder. Der Kanton Glarus ist der südlichste Kanton, der noch zur Tourismusregion Ostschweiz gehört. Lange Täler und hohe Berge machen den Reiz dieser Landschaft aus. Hier endet die Reise in unserm Buch.

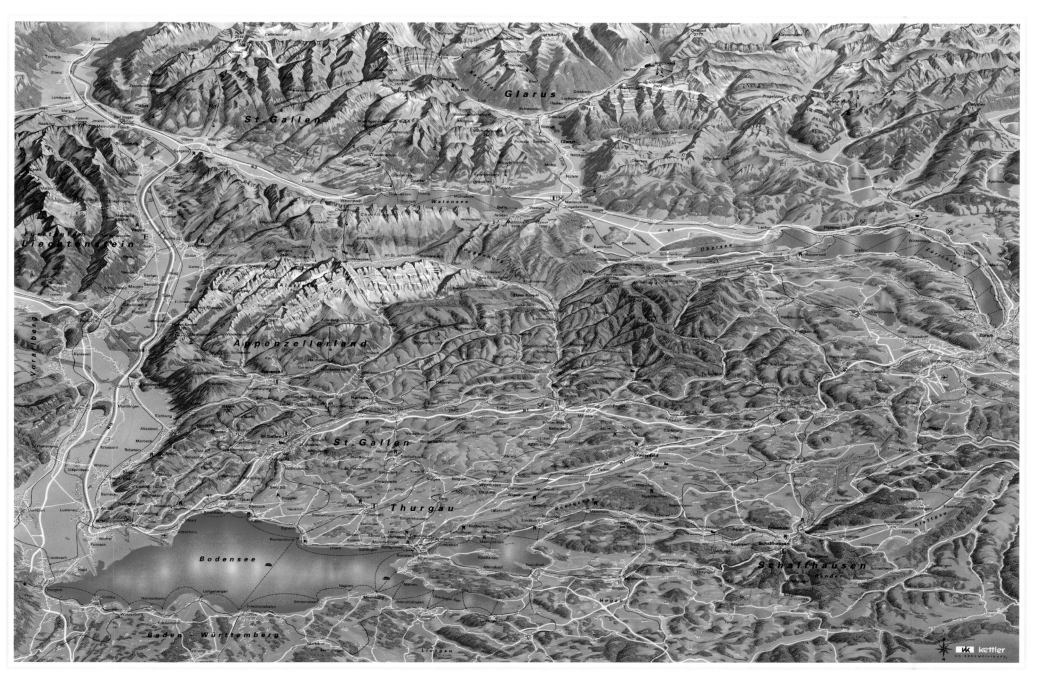

Panoramakarte Ostschweiz

Stein am Rhein

Insel Werd bei Stein am Rhein

Hallau im Klettgau

Rheinfall bei Schaffhausen

Munot, Schaffhausen

Diessenhofen

Arenenberg am Untersee

Berlingen am Untersee

Berlingen am Untersee

Steckborn am Untersee

Kreuzlingen und Konstanz am Bodensee

Schloss Frauenfeld

Kartause Ittingen

Thurberg bei Weinfelden

Fischingen im Hinterthurgau

Im Thurgau bei Wertbüel

Hagenwil

Wasserschloss Hagenwil

Raddampfer Hohentwiel

Romanshorn am Bodensee

Arbon am Bodensee

Fischer auf dem Bodensee

Arbon am Bodensee

Fischmarktplatz Arbon

Bodensee, Segelboot im Sturm

Steinach am Bodensee

Im Thurgau bei Roggwil

Thurgauer Riegelhäuser in Roggwil

Sitterbrücke bei Bischofszell

St. Pelagiberg

Seenachtfest

Abendstimmung am Bodensee

Hauptwil

Gallusplatz, St.Gallen

Schmiedgasse, St.Gallen

St.Gallen

Klosterhof, St. Gallen

St.Gallen

Wil

Rorschach am Bodensee

Föhnmorgen am Bodensee

Beim Eggli, Marwees, Altmann, Ebenalp

Appenzell mit Säntis

Schlatt

Appenzellerbauernhaus

Wasserauen, Schwende mit Marwees und Ebenalp

Dorfplatz in Urnäsch

Alpstein, Fälensee, Kreuzberge, Altmann, Säntis

Morgenstimmung auf dem Säntis

Alter Säntis

Panoramaaussicht auf dem Säntis

Nebelmeer über dem Mittelland

Stauberenchanzlen

Hoher Kasten, Sämtisersee, Alpstein

Seealpsee

Äscher beim Wildkirchli, Alpstein mit Marwees

Alp Sigel, Saxerlücke und Kreuzberge

Hochalp mit Säntis

Auf dem Weg zur Viehschau

Viehschau

Kuh

Stein

Kronberg, Scheidegg

Appenzellerland, Säntis bei Schwellbrunn

Teufen

Bei Appenzell, Schlatt

Appenzeller Bauernhäuser bei Stein

"Bloch" Traditioneller Brauch

"Schön-wüeschti" Silvesterkläuse

Schöner Silvesterklaus

Alp Sigel, Nebel über Wasserauen

Schwägalp, Säntis

Trogen

Lutertannen

Winterabend bei Stein

Haslen

Dorfplatz Gais

Stein mit Hundwiler Höhi

Grub mit Sicht auf den Bodensee

Heiden

Grabserberg, Margelchopf

Werdenberg

Bei Wildhaus, Churfirsten

Wildhaus

Magdenau

Toggenburger Bauernhaus

Altstätten im St.Galler Rheintal

St.Galler Rheintal mit Widnau, Heerbrugg, Bodensee

Schloss Vaduz mit Sicht ins St.Galleroberland

Schloss Vaduz im Fürstentum Liechtenstein

Bei Grabs im St.Galler Rheintal

Sargans

Rapperswil

Schwägalppass vom Toggenburg mit Alpstein, Säntis

Taminaschlucht bei Bad Ragaz

Pizol

Amden

Weesen am Walensee, Sicht ins Glarnerland

Walensee

Quinten am Walensee

Bei Mollis, Wiggis und Rautispitz

Aussicht vom Kerenzerberg ins Glarnerland

Glarus mit Vrenelisgärtli

Obersee, Brünnelistock

Linthtal, Tödi

Braunwald, Ortstock

Auf Wiedersehen...
Good bye...